Could war erupt over Taiwan?

The Role of America in Beijing and Taiwan's differences

Interests

The players

The Gainers

The Losers

Bruce S. Peterson

Table of Contents

Prologue

U.S. analysts are particularly concerned that a confrontation could break out as a result of China's expanding military might and aggression, as well as the worsening in relations across the Taiwan Strait. A confrontation between the United States and China could result from such a conflict. That's because both China and the United States haven't ruled out using force to bring about Taiwan's "reunification" if China attacks. The People's Liberation Army (PLA) of China is "likely preparing for a contingency to unify Taiwan with the PRC by force, while simultaneously deterring, delaying, or denying any third-party intervention, such as the United States," according to a 2021 report from the U.S. Department of Defense.

However, experts disagree about the likelihood and timing of a Chinese invasion. Although some experts think that such an invasion is still a ways off, the top U.S. military commander in the Indo-Pacific warned in 2021 that China might try to invade Taiwan within the following ten years. Others think 2049 is a crucial year; Xi has underlined that Taiwan's unification is necessary to realize what he calls the Chinese Dream, which calls for the restoration of China's great-power status by 2049.

Early in 2022, Russia invaded Ukraine, reigniting the debate. Some analysts claimed that Moscow's actions might give Beijing the confidence to invade Taiwan similarly, while others claimed that Beijing might become more cautious after seeing Russia's difficulties. China's inclination to use force won't be affected by Russia's actions, according to CFR's Sacks, who also writes that "Chinese officials will review Russia's failings and alter their operational plans to avoid making similar mistakes."

Regardless, the PLA has made preparing for a Taiwan contingency one of its top priorities, and Taiwan has been a major catalyst for China's military modernization. In a 2019 defence white paper, the PLA said it would "resolutely defeat anyone attempting to separate Taiwan from China."

Without assistance from elsewhere, researchers believe Taiwan cannot repel a Chinese assault. Even though Tsai and the DPP have made boosting defence spending a priority and have allocated a budget record of about $17 billion for 2022, China is still thought to spend about twenty-two times as much on defence as Taiwan. Taiwanese lawmakers gave their approval to the Tsai administration's plan to increase defence spending by $8.6 billion over the following five years in 2022. To protect Taiwan's coasts, a portion of this increased military budget will be used to purchase cruise missiles, marine mines, and cutting-edge surveillance systems.

The present Status quo

Taiwan also referred to as the Republic of China (ROC), is an island situated across the Taiwan Strait from mainland China. Since 1949, it has been run separately from the rest of China as the People's Republic of China (PRC). The PRC declares that Taiwan will one day "unify" with the mainland and sees the island as a renegade province. Political leaders in Taiwan, an island nation with a democratically elected government and a population of 23 million, hold contrasting opinions about the status of the island and its ties to the mainland.

Cross-strait tensions have escalated since the election of Taiwanese President Tsai Ing-wen in 2016. Tsai has refused to accept a formula that her predecessor, Ma Ying-jeou, endorsed to allow for increased cross-strait ties. Meanwhile, Beijing has taken increasingly aggressive actions, including flying fighter jets near the island. Some analysts fear a Chinese attack on Taiwan has the potential to draw the United States into a war with China.

Is Taiwan part of China?

Beijing asserts that there is only "one China" and that Taiwan is part of it. It views the PRC as the only legitimate government of China, an approach it calls the One-China principle and seeks Taiwan's eventual "unification" with the mainland.

Beijing claims that Taiwan is limited by a comprehension known as the 1992 Consensus, which was reached between agents of the Chinese Communist Party (CCP) and the Kuomintang (KMT) party that then managed Taiwan. In any case, the different sides disagree on the substance of this purported agreement, and resolving the subject of Taiwan's legitimate status was rarely expected. For the PRC, as Chinese President Xi Jinping has expressed, the 1992 Consensus mirrors an arrangement that "the different sides of the waterway have a place with one China and would cooperate to look for public reunification." For the KMT, it signifies "one China, various translations," with the ROC remaining as the "one China."

Taiwan's KMT-drafted constitution keeps on perceiving China, Mongolia, Taiwan, Tibet, and the South China Sea as a component of the ROC. The KMT doesn't uphold Taiwan's autonomy and has reliably called for nearer attaches with Beijing. However, notwithstanding late political race misfortunes, KMT pioneers have talked about whether to change the party's position on the 1992 Consensus.

The KMT's central adversary party, the Democratic Progressive Party (DPP), has never supported the figuring out spread out in the 1992 Consensus. President Tsai, who is likewise the head of the DPP, has declined to acknowledge the agreement unequivocally. All things being equal, she has endeavoured to find another detailing that would be satisfactory to Beijing. In her 2016 debut address, Tsai noted she was "chosen president as per the Constitution of the Republic of China," which is a one-China report, and said she would "defend the power and domain of the Republic of China." Tsai likewise swore that she would "lead cross-waterway undertakings as per the Republic of China Constitution, the Act Governing Relations Between the People of [the] Taiwan Area and the Mainland Area, and other important regulations." Beijing, nonetheless, dismissed this plan and cut off true contacts with Taiwan.

In a 2019 discourse, Xi emphasized China's well-established proposition for Taiwan: that it be integrated into the central area under the recipe of "one country, two frameworks." This is a similar equation utilized for Hong Kong, which ensured the capacity to safeguard its political and financial frameworks and conceded a "serious level of independence." Such a structure is profoundly disliked among the Taiwanese public. Highlighting Beijing's new crackdown on Hong Kong's opportunities, Tsai and, surprisingly, the KMT has dismissed the "one country, two frameworks" structure.

TAIWAN AT A GLANCE

Area	35,980 square kilometres (slightly smaller than Maryland and Delaware combined)
Form of Government	Semi presidential republic
Population	24 million (2022)
GDP	$774 billion (2021)
GDP per capita	$33,004 (2021)
Life Expectancy	81 years (2022)
Religions	Buddhism 35%, Taoism 33%, Christianity 4%, folk 10%, none or unspecified 18% (2005)
Languages	Mandarin Chinese (official), Minnan, Hakka dialects, Indigenous languages

Is Taiwan a member of the United Nations?

No. China dismisses Taiwan's cooperation as a part of UN offices and other worldwide associations that limit enrollment to states. Taipei routinely fights its prohibition; the United States likewise pushes for Taiwan's significant cooperation in such associations. Amid the COVID-19 pandemic, Taipei condemned the World Health Organization (WHO) for yielding to Beijing's requests and proceeding to bar Taiwan — which mounted one of the world's best reactions to COVID-19 in the initial two years of the pandemic — from going to the association's World Health Assembly as a spectator. Clergymen from the Group of Seven (G7) nations have required Taiwan's consideration in WHO gatherings.

Taiwan does, in any case, hold part status over forty associations, a large portion of them territorial, for example, the Asian Development Bank and the Asia-Pacific Economic Cooperation gathering, as well as the World Trade Organization. It holds spectator or another status on a few different bodies.

Just fourteen states keep up with true discretionary binds with Taiwan. No administration has at any point the while keeping up with formal political binds with both China and Taiwan.

What is the United States' relationship with Taiwan?

In 1979, the United States laid out formal strategic relations with the PRC. Simultaneously, it cut off its conciliatory ties and revoked its peace accord with the ROC. In any case, the United States keeps a powerful informal relationship with the island and keeps on offering guard hardware to its military. Beijing has over and again encouraged Washington to quit offering weapons and stop contact with Taipei.

The U.S. approach is administered by its One-China strategy. It depends on a few records, like three U.S.- China reports came to in 1972, 1978, and 1982; the Taiwan Relations Act, passed by the U.S. Congress in 1979; and the late declassified "Six Assurances", which President Ronald Reagan passed on to Taiwan in 1982. These records spread out that the United States: "recognizes the Chinese place that there is nevertheless one China and Taiwan is important for China" and that the PRC is the "sole legitimate legislature of China" (some U.S. authorities have underscored that the utilization of "recognize" suggests that the United States doesn't be guaranteed to acknowledge the Chinese position); dismisses any utilization of power to resolve the debate; keeps up with social, business, and different binds with Taiwan, brought out through the American Institute in Taiwan (AIT); focuses on offering arms to Taiwan for self-preservation; and will keep up with the capacity to come to Taiwan's protection, while not focusing on doing so — a strategy known as essential equivocalness.

The United States central objective is to keep up with harmony and strength in the Taiwan Strait, and it has begged both Beijing and Taipei to keep up with the state of affairs. It says it doesn't uphold Taiwanese autonomy.

Through its strategy of key equivocalness, the United States has for a long time endeavoured to keep a sensitive harmony between supporting Taiwan and forestalling a conflict with China. However, President Joe Biden has dismissed the arrangement, expressing a few times that the United States would come to Taiwan's protection assuming China went after it. White House authorities have strolled back his remarks, saying the approach has not changed, at the end of the day, the president will choose how to answer. A few specialists, like CFR's Richard Haass and David Sacks, and a few individuals from Congress have invited Biden's explanations, contending that China's expanded hostility requires clearness. Different specialists have contradicted this position.

How have recent U.S. administrations approached Taiwan?

Under President Donald Trump, the United States extended its attaches with Taiwan over Chinese protests, including by selling more than $18 billion worth of arms to the military and uncovering a $250 million complex for its true consulate in Taipei. Trump talked with Tsai by phone in front of his introduction, the most elevated level of contact between the different sides starting around 1979. He likewise sent a few senior organization authorities — including a bureau part — to Taipei, and during his last days in office, the State Department dispensed with long-held limitations overseeing where and how U.S. authorities can meet with their Taiwanese partners.

The Biden organization has adopted a comparable strategy, proceeding with arms deals and insisting on the Trump organization's choice to permit U.S. authorities to meet all the more unreservedly with Taiwanese authorities. Biden was the primary U.S. president to welcome Taiwanese agents to go to the official introduction. The United States takes part in military preparation and exchanges with Taiwan, consistently cruises ships through the Taiwan Strait to show its tactical presence in the district, and has urged Taiwan to expand its guard spending.

Additionally, Taiwan has gotten bipartisan help in Congress throughout the long term, with officials proposing and passing regulations to support U.S.-

Taiwan relations, reinforce the island's guards, and energize its cooperation in global associations. The most recent proposed regulation, the Taiwan Policy Act of 2022 [PDF], incorporates assigning Taiwan as a significant non-North Atlantic Treaty Organization (NATO) partner. In August 2022, House Speaker Nancy Pelosi (D-CA) visited Taipei — the main speaker to do as such since Newt Gingrich (R-GA) in 1997 — and met with Tsai. Beijing firmly censured the visit and accordingly arranged military activities that successfully encompass the island and prohibited imports of a few leafy foods from Taiwan, among different activities.

U.S. Military Support for Taiwan: What's Changed Under Trump?

The Trump organization made strong motions on the side of Taiwan, including more regular development of U.S. ships in the Taiwan Strait. They came during a period of developing nervousness about the U.S.- China relationship.

For a considerable length of time, U.S. military boats cruised through the Taiwan Strait, as a demonstration of help for Taipei and a test for Beijing. They are only one part of the Trump organization's support for Taiwan and joined with China's more forceful way to deal with the popularity-based island, numerous investigators dread a cross-waterway emergency.

Besides military contacts, President Donald J. Trump has reinforced Taiwan through different measures. After the 2016 political decision, for instance, he conversed with Taiwanese President Tsai Ing-wen on the telephone in what was accepted to be the initial time a U.S. president or president-elect talked straightforwardly with a Taiwanese chief since no less than 1979. In 2018, the United States uncovered $250 million worth of moves up to a true consulate in Taipei regardless of Chinese protests.

While the Trump organization made more decisive strides than those of its ancestors, its arms deals with Taiwan are so far nothing amazing.

The United States has offered military hardware to Taiwan starting around 1979. That year, as President Jimmy Carter cut off formal discretionary binds with the island and officially perceived China, Congress passed the Taiwan Relations Act, which is the reason for Washington's relationship with Taipei and incorporates the arrangement of arms for Taiwan's self-protection. The law doesn't need the United States to guard Taiwan if China assaults, yet it likewise doesn't preclude it — a strategy known as essential vagueness.

From that point forward, the United States has finished its obligation to help the island's protections, with Taiwan positioned as one of the top shippers of U.S. arms lately. During his initial term, President Barack Obama approved two significant bundles, adding up to about $12 billion [PDF]. President George W. Shrub supported nine arms bundles, worth around $5 billion, during his initial term.

Trump reported two significant military deals with Taiwan. The first, supported in June 2017, was valued at $1.4 billion and included progressed rockets and torpedoes. It likewise offered specialized help for an early-advance notice radar framework. In October 2018, a subsequent arms bundle, worth an expected $330 million, was supported.

A Cross-Strait Crisis Looming?

The mists over Taiwan have developed hazier as of late. In January, Chinese President Xi Jinping said Taiwan should be bound together with the central area and asked Taipei to embrace the 1992 Consensus. It expresses that there is as it were "one China" and Taiwan has a place with it however permits various understandings of which is the overseeing substance. China "won't preclude the utilization of power" against unfamiliar intercession, Xi said. Tsai emphasized that her administration won't ever acknowledge the "one country, two frameworks" model and protected the popularity-based island's power.

The troubling China-Taiwan pressures come as the U.S.- China relationship has disintegrated, with the two opponents taking part in significant disagreements regarding exchange and innovation and bumping for power in the western Pacific. During the current week's North Atlantic Treaty Organization (NATO) gatherings in Washington, dangers from China were highlighted more conspicuously than at any time in recent memory.

Specialists express these elements are expanding the gamble of a cross-waterway emergency. "Business as usual is defective," composed CFR President Richard N. Haass, "yet it is undeniably less defective than what might follow one-sided activities and endeavours to determine what is happening that doesn't fit a flawless arrangement.".

Could war erupt over Taiwan?

A top concern among U.S. analysts is that China's growing military capabilities and assertiveness, as well as the deterioration in cross-strait relations, could spark a conflict. Such a conflict has the potential to lead to a U.S.-China confrontation. That's because China hasn't ruled out using force to achieve Taiwan's "reunification" and the United States hasn't ruled out defending Taiwan if China attacks. The U.S. Department Of Defense said in a 2021 report that China's military, the People's Liberation Army (PLA), is "likely preparing for a contingency to unify Taiwan with the PRC by force, while simultaneously deterring, delaying, or denying any third-party intervention, such as the United States."

Be that as it may, specialists differ about the probability and timing of a Chinese intrusion. The top U.S. military commandant in the Indo-Pacific cautioned in 2021 that China could attempt to attack Taiwan inside the following decade], while certain specialists accept that such an attack is further off. Others accept that 2049 is a basic date; Xi has underscored that unification with Taiwan is fundamental to accomplishing what he calls the Chinese Dream, which sees China's extraordinary power status reestablished by 2049.

Russia's attack on Ukraine in mid-2022 reignited the discussion, for certain examiners contending that Moscow's moves could encourage Beijing to correspondingly attack Taiwan and others saying that Beijing could turn out to be warier after seeing Russia's difficulties. CFR's Sacks composes that Russia's activities won't impact China's eagerness to utilize force, yet that "Chinese pioneers will analyze Russia's disappointments and adjust their functional designs to try not to commit comparative errors."

Notwithstanding, the PLA has made getting ready for a Taiwan possibility one of its main concerns, and Taiwan has been a significant impetus for China's tactical modernization. In a 2019 guard white paper, the PLA said it would "unflinchingly rout anybody endeavouring to isolate Taiwan from China."

Taiwan probably can't guard against a Chinese assault without outer help, examiners say. Even though Tsai and the DPP have focused on expanding protection spending, with a record financial plan of almost $17 billion for 2022, China's spending is as yet assessed to associate with multiple times Taiwan's. In 2022, Taiwanese legislators supported the Tsai government's arrangement to spend an extra $8.6 billion on protection over the following five years. Some portion of this extended military spending plan will go toward procuring journey rockets, maritime mines, and high-level reconnaissance frameworks to safeguard Taiwan's coasts.

How has China tried to intimidate Taiwan?

China has utilized various coercive strategies shy of outfitted struggle, and it has sloped up these actions since Tsai's political decision in 2016. Its goal is to wear out Taiwan and brief the islanders' to reason that their most ideal choice is unification with the central area. With that in mind, China has expanded the recurrence and size of watches of PLA planes, contender planes, and reconnaissance aeroplanes over and around Taiwan. It has additionally progressively cruised its warships and plane-carrying warships through the Taiwan Strait in shows of power.

Taiwan has announced that a great many cyberattacks from China focus on its administration organizations consistently. These assaults have taken off lately. In 2020, Taipei blamed four Chinese gatherings for hacking into no less than ten Taiwanese government organizations and 6,000 authority email accounts starting around 2018 to attempt to get government information and individual data.

Beijing has additionally utilized nonmilitary measures to pressure Taiwan. In 2016, China suspended a cross-waterway correspondence system with the principal Taiwan contact office. It confined the travel industry to Taiwan, and the number of central area vacationers visiting Taiwan tumbled from a high of the north of 4 million in 2015 to 2.7 million in 2019. China has likewise constrained worldwide organizations, including carriers and lodging networks, to list Taiwan as Chinese territory. Likewise, China has scared nations that have attached tooan: in 2021, China cut off trade with Lithuania for opening a Taiwanese delegate office in its capital.

Has Beijing undermined Taiwan's democracy?

Notwithstanding the strategies depicted above, China has sloped up impedance in Taiwan's races. Its techniques remember spreading disinformation for virtual entertainment and expanding its command over Taiwanese news sources. In the 2020 political race, for instance, China spread disinformation in an obvious work to harm Tsai and support the KMT's official applicant. Such endeavours are important for China's bigger procedure of utilizing pressure to disintegrate trust in Taiwan's political framework and sow divisions in Taiwanese society. Be that as it may, specialists view the DPP's progress in late races, remembering Tsai's re-appointment for 2020, as a censure of Beijing.

Taiwan's majority rules system is moderately youthful. The KMT was administered under military regulation from 1949 to 1987. During that time, the political dispute was cruelly quelled and the Taiwanese who had long occupied the island before 1945 confronted segregation. Taiwan held its most memorable free official races in 1992 and its most memorable official decisions in 1996. From that point forward, it has calmly moved power between parties a few times.

Regardless of Chinese dangers, Taiwan seems to have up until this point evaded the pattern of apostatizing and distressing popular governments all over the planet. In 2020, the Economist's Democracy Index named Taiwan a "full majority rule government" interestingly. In 2021, Taiwan was positioned as the world's eighth-most-popularity-based country. That is higher than its Asian neighbours (South Korea positioned sixteenth and Japan positioned seventeenth) and the United States, which positioned twenty-6th. Late races have seen high citizen turnout.

Do Taiwanese people support independence?

The vast majority in Taiwan support keeping up with the state of affairs. A modest number help prompt freedom, as indicated by assessments of public sentiment directed by National Chengchi University. Considerably less express help for the unification of Taiwan with China. A mind-boggling greater part rejects a "one country, two frameworks" model, an opinion that has developed as Beijing takes action against Hong Kong's opportunities.

A rising number of Taiwanese individuals feel more intently attached to Taiwan than to the central area. Over 62% of the island's occupants viewed themselves as only Taiwanese in 2021, a review by National Chengchi University found. By examination, 32% were recognized as both Taiwanese and Chinese, down from 40% 10 years sooner. Something like 3% viewed themselves as just Chinese, a figure that has diminished beginning around 1994 when 26 per cent recognized that way.

What is Taiwan's economic situation?

Taiwan's economy remains reliant on trade with China, which is the island's largest trading partner. However, their economic relationship has experienced disruptions in recent years, partly due to Beijing's pressure on the island and Taiwanese officials' growing concern about its overreliance on trade with China.

Under President Ma, who was in office from 2008 to 2016, Taiwan marked more than twenty settlements with the PRC, including the 2010 Cross-Straits Economic Cooperation Framework Agreement [PDF], where they consented to lift boundaries to exchange. China and Taiwan continued direct ocean, air, and mail interfaces that had been restricted for a long time. They additionally consented to permit banks, guarantors, and other monetary specialist organizations to work in the two business sectors.

Tsai and the DPP, then again, have endeavoured to enhance Taiwan's exchange connections, with blended results. Tsai has had some achievements supporting exchange with adventurous nations in Southeast Asia and the Indo-Pacific through a marked drive, the New Southbound Policy. Exchange among Taiwan and the eighteen designated nations expanded by more than $50 billion between 2016, when the drive was divulged, and 2021. Taiwanese interest in those nations has additionally consistently expanded. In 2019, Tsai uncovered a three-year plan to boost Taiwanese producers to move from the central area back to Taiwan.

In any case, in 2021, Taiwan's products to China hit an unsurpassed high. Beijing has compelled nations not to consent to streamlined commerce arrangements with Taiwan. A modest bunch of nations have marked deregulation settlements with the island; New Zealand and Singapore are the main created economies to consent to such arrangements. Beijing has likewise pushed for Taiwan's prohibition from multilateral exchanging alliances, including the Comprehensive and Progressive Agreement for Trans-Pacific Partnership (CPTPP) and the Regional Comprehensive Economic Partnership (RCEP). (China is remembered for the RCEP yet not in the CPTPP.) Taiwan likewise isn't essential for the Biden organization's Indo-Pacific Economic Framework.

Have cross-strait tensions hurt Taiwan's vital semiconductor chip manufacturers?

Taiwan is the world's top contract manufacturer of semiconductor chips, and its industry is booming despite cross-strait tensions. These chips are found in most electronics, including smartphones, computers, vehicles, and even weapons systems that rely on artificial intelligence. Companies in Taiwan were responsible for more than 60 per cent of the revenue generated by the world's semiconductor contract manufacturers in 2020.

Quite a bit of that can be credited to Taiwan Semiconductor Manufacturing Company (TSMC), the world's biggest agreement chip creator and the top provider for Apple and other U.S. organizations. It is one of just two organizations on the planet (the other is South Korea-based Samsung) that has the mechanical expertise to make the littlest, most developed chips, and it fabricates more than 90% of them.

A few specialists contend that the United States' reliance on Taiwanese chip firms elevates its inspiration to protect Taiwan from a Chinese assault. Perceiving the degree to which the United States depends on one organization for basic chips, Biden has pushed to reinforce the U.S. chip industry; in 2022, Congress passed a general $280 billion bill to do as such. China likewise depends on Taiwanese chips, however not hogwash as the United States does. Beijing is attempting to support its industry, particularly as Washington has pushed TSMC to quit offering to Chinese organizations, including Huawei, a

Chinese media communications goliath that Washington claims Beijing could use for undercover work.

Why Taiwan Strait important?

In the advanced world, it is the entryway utilized by boats of pretty much every benevolent on a section to and from essentially every one of the significant ports in Northeast Asia. In 2020 Chinese vessels had been illicitly fishing and digging sand on the Taiwanese portion of the waterway. Taiwan is building significant breeze ranches in the waterway.

The Taiwan Strait is a 180-kilometre (110 mi; 97 mi)- wide waterway isolating the island of Taiwan and mainland Asia. The waterway is essential for the South China Sea and associated with the East China Sea toward the north. The tightest part is 130 km (81 mi; 70 mi) wide.

Summary

Taiwan has been represented autonomously by China beginning around 1949, however, Beijing sees the island as a feature of its domain. Beijing has promised to ultimately "bring together" Taiwan with the central area, utilizing force if important.

Strains are rising. Taiwanese President Tsai Ing-wen, whose party stage favours freedom, has reprimanded Beijing's endeavours to subvert a majority-rule government. Beijing has sloped up political and military strain on Taipei.

A few investigators dread that the United States and China could do battle over Taiwan. U.S. House Speaker Nancy Pelosi's outing to the island in 2022 elevated strains between the nations.